SPIT &
POLISH

*Old-fashioned Ways
to Banish Dirt, Dust
and Decay*

LUCY LETHBRIDGE

BLOOMSBURY
LONDON · OXFORD · NEW YORK · NEW DELHI · SYDNEY

Bloomsbury Publishing
An imprint of Bloomsbury Publishing Plc

50 Bedford Square
London, WC1B 3DP, UK

1385 Broadway
New York, NY 10018, USA

www.bloomsbury.com

BLOOMSBURY and the Diana logo are trademarks of Bloomsbury Publishing Plc

First published in Great Britain 2016

British Library Cataloguing-in-Publication Data
A catalogue record for this book is available from the British Library.

ISBN: HB: 978-1-4088-6642-9
ePub: 978-1-4088-6644-3

2 4 6 8 10 9 7 5 3 1

Typeset by Newgen Knowledge Works (P) Ltd., Chennai, India
Printed and bound in China by C&C Offset Printing Co. Ltd

To find out more about our authors and books visit www.bloomsbury.com. Here you
will find extracts, author interviews, details of forthcoming events and the option to
sign up for our newsletters.

For Sarah Cole, whose idea it was

CONTENTS

Introduction

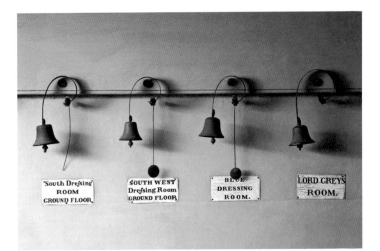

Domestic business is no less demanding
for being less important
Montaigne

I N 1900, GENERAL HOUSEWORK in the British home
was so labour intensive that it required a workforce
of servants to implement it. This in turn entrenched a
hierarchy of exacting standards of cleanliness, etiquette
and order that made it impossible for the middle-class
family to imagine being without domestic help. Taking
their inspiration from the upper-class country household, with its fleets of uniformed and liveried retainers,
middle-class homeowners financially crippled themselves to afford even a single maid rather than suffer the
ignominy of doing their own housework.

The more furnished, padded, well stocked and decorat-
ed homes became, the more housework they generated.
A profusion of cheap, factory-made fabrics resulted in
more laundry, more furniture meant more dusting, the
increase in available foodstuffs meant elaborate meals
and more washing up. The outside world was dirtier (or
rather the dirt, in the form of dust, smuts and mud, was

more visible) than it is today. Geoffrey Brady, who was born in 1898, lived in an affluent suburb of Stockport. He remembered the constant labour of the family's servants: 'If you had your windows open for quarter of an hour you had to go round with a duster afterwards to clean up the smuts and things like that. Curtains were being washed continuously and one's clothes and handkerchiefs were quite filthy by the end of the day.'

Technology has followed domestic labour, finding ways to speed up and alleviate household tasks. By the 1880s, there seemed to be a device, with varying degrees of real usefulness, for every requirement. 'No matter whether we desire to clean knives or make stockings, peel potatoes, black shoes, make butter, wash clothes, stitch dresses, shell peas or even make our bread, all we have to do is turn a handle. This is a regular handle-turning age,' wrote a correspondent in the 1882 *Journal of Domestic Appliances*. Mangles, knife-cleaners, boot-polishers, dishwashers, vacuum cleaners – all these reduce the labour of the business of keeping clean; though it is interesting to note that machinery sometimes actually expands the number of hours put into housework. Washing machines enable us nowadays to wash our clothes a great deal more often than the old days when there was one weekly laundry.

Advances in household technology vied with a longer-standing resistance to the idea of 'labour-saving'. Work was morally uplifting – particularly when you weren't the one doing it. Old-fashioned servants remembered how employers looked for signs of physical labour and suffering as indications of a job well

done. 'Now Edith, you're getting lazy', admonished Edith Hall's employer in the 1920s, when she wanted to use a soapy water wash for cleaning the floor rather than the harsh soda and water concoction that hardened hands and burned the colour off the linoleum. However, for many others the rise in popularity of new branded detergents and household cleaners such as 'Sunlight' and 'Lifebuoy' gave a whole new definition to the meaning of clean. It was not enough for an object to simply be without a coating of dirt – now it had to smell of the powder it had been washed in.

Following the technologies available to us, our idea of everyday cleanliness has changed radically over the last hundred years or so. Few people now would think it extravagant to change their clothes every day or to take a daily bath – but they probably only rarely wash their skirting boards or dust down their books. The piney, lemony smells of detergents can mask any nasty odours and a quick spray round the kitchen with a disinfectant or an anti-bacterial liquid feels as though it has probably done the business regarding lurking germs. Our kitchen tables and surfaces, covered in Formica or some other easy-wipe sealant, are far easier to keep clean than the daily scrubbing of stained and pitted pitch pine tables that was the lot of the kitchen maid.

Nevertheless, we can still learn much from the old-fashioned household skills employed by career servants. No Edwardian maid would have been stumped by a wax-covered brass candlestick or a dirty, faded rug. The chemical components of a housemaid's cupboard seem today like a terrifyingly toxic laboratory. In fact, a few basic components – either acid or alkali, depending – formed the basis of almost all cleaning. It is quite unnecessary to buy a special bathroom spray to protect against mildew if you have a bottle of white vinegar to hand which will do the job just as well for half the price. Tea leaves for sweeping carpets, lemon juice for cleaning copper, boiling water and bicarbonate of soda are some of the basic ingredients that once cleaned a house. In this book I have gathered nearly two centuries of cleaning tips from the memoirs of servants themselves, from housekeeping guides and advice manuals. This book covers every corner of the house, from dusting ceilings to clearing drains and getting rid of cockroaches. The best and simplest of older methods still work for us today – and in many cases their modern equivalents are simply variants of them. These tips are, for the most part, quick; they are also cheap, environmentally friendly and effective.

1

The Household Cupboard

59, HOLBORN HILL.

The omnium gatherum of the house
J. B. Alden, 1880

A N IMPRESSIVE VARIETY OF INGENIOUS materials have been used for cleaning over the centuries. The average cleaning cupboard today will probably contain little more than a vacuum cleaner, some kind of mop and a broom; maybe also a few dusters and some liquid cleaning solution. But a century ago, a household cupboard, even in a modest home, would have contained a piece of equipment for every conceivable domestic task – all arrayed in the 'orderly manner' recommended by Mrs Beeton in her first *Book of Household Management*.

The authors of manuals of servants' duties always stress the importance of the tidiness and order of this cupboard. It was, as Mrs Beeton put it, 'where perfect order should prevail': it was seen as a reflection of the order of the house, and therefore of the psychological order of its occupants. The housekeeper had charge of cleaning materials in larger homes, and in smaller houses, the housemaid's closet, usually on an upper landing, was the centre of operations. This sometimes had its own supply of soft water pumped in from the outside. Most housekeeping experts recommended that the closet contained a small copper (a built-in copper-lined container with a fire beneath it for boiling water). Generally found

> ## TIP!
>
> KEEP A BULK SUPPLY OF CHEAP HOUSEHOLD SALT: it has a multitude of uses outside cooking. Adding a teaspoon of salt to a vase of flowers, for example, will keep them fresh longer.
>
>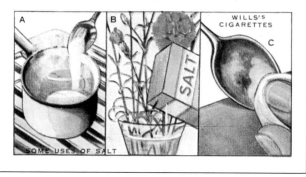

near the servants' bedrooms on the top floor, the closet also usually contained a sink where the contents of the household's chamber-pots were disposed of every morning. The surrounding area therefore tended to be, as the *Hand Book of House Sanitation* warned in 1882, 'subject to a slight though disagreeable odour'.

Water, however, was not in general as integral to household cleaning as it is today. Methods had to be found that limited the use of water in homes that, even with some rudimentary plumbing, had far less access to it than we have today. In the mid-nineteenth century, until the implementation of the reforms recommended by Edwin Chadwick's 1842 report on sanitary conditions in urban slums, for the city-dwelling poor, water was available only from professional water carriers (who charged high prices) or from shared public pumps.

The labour of carrying, heating and disposing of water meant it could not be used recklessly: three tons a week was the average weight in water carried by a single maid in a modest house in the 1890s. This went for bodily cleanliness too: until the development of plumbed bathrooms in the late nineteenth and early twentieth centuries, bathing was infrequent and vigorous dry brushing or rubbing with a rough cloth was an effective means of shifting dirt.

The average nineteenth-century cleaning cupboard featured a vast array of brushes (*see* p. 14), as well as supplies of soap of all varieties, scourers, polishers and rags. It also housed a variety of cloths, each type carefully sorted into piles. There would be mountains of soft flannel, often made from worn-out nightdresses, and a great many scraps and rags of cotton or muslin. Cloths made of 'scrim', a coarsely woven flax or cotton material, were useful for cleaning windows; thinner cheesecloths were for dusting; and of course chamois leather was used for buffing and polishing.

Brushes

There were coconut fibre brushes for carpets; soft brushes for textiles and woodwork; retractable brushes for the top of curtains and spider brushes for cobwebs. There were plate brushes, horsehair blacking brushes, clothes brushes (hard and soft), bottle-brushes, water brushes (for corners of the skirting where a mop can't get a purchase) and flexible brushes for getting hair-plugs out of drains. There were brushes for shoes (for putting on polish, for removing it, then for buffing up the shine); small soft ones for kid gloves; bristlier ones to get dried mud off hems. An old-fashioned chandelier duster was called a 'Turk's head' and, according to butler Stanley Ager, looked like a 'soldier's busby on the end of a pole'.

Feather dusters were made from cocks' tail feathers, 'camel-hair' clothes brushes from squirrel fur. A rural tradition was using cockscombs for the tricky work of cleaning chimney flues as the rubbery flanges dug into corners.

Journalist Mrs Alfred Praga suggested in her *Start-ing Housekeeping* (1900) that the starter household could keep cleaning chemicals to what she considered a minimum: 'Here is a list of the things you will actually

need: Carbolic soap, yellow soap, and your favourite brand of that commodity in a powdered and put-up-in packet state; powdered pumice stone, in conjunction with paraffin or kerosene, the latter for preference, to be used to remove stains from the marble-topped wash-stands &c, should any exist; Benzine [a by-product of the distillation of petroleum and used to help dissolve fat and resin], for better cleaning of paint &c; metal polish for the brasses and coppers ... Soda [a compound of sodium, an alkali] of course you must have: black-lead, emery paper [sandpaper], both the coarse and fine varieties, soft soap, beeswax and turpentine – the latter bought ready mixed – furniture cream or polish for those articles which do not lend themselves amiably to bees-waxing, and a large bottle of your favourite disinfectant for flushing sinks, &c.'

HOUSEHOLD CLEANERS were purchased by the hundred-weight and delivered to the door in wooden tubs ('about the size of a two-gallon barrel', remembered Stanley Ager). Soap, such as Fairy, a green soft soap made with olive oil, came in enormous bars that were then cut to size as required, or grated into water to make a jelly. Since the 1890s, branded carbolic soaps, such as Lifebuoy or Wright's, which contained strong-smelling, disinfecting coal tar, were popular, as was Lever Brothers' Sunlight, recommended for washing dishes and laundry.

Other cleaning materials included ammonia, a strong alkali and mild bleaching agent used as a solvent for grease and paint stains (and sometimes known as harts-horn because in its original form, it came from the calcined antlers of a deer). Borax, a salt derived from the combination of boracid acid and soda, was used as a grease solvent, water-softener and antiseptic, and should still be an indispensable part of the cleaning armoury. Castile soap was a gentle soap made from olive oil. Castor oil, made from the beans of the castor oil plant, was kept for nourishing leather (and sometimes children). Chloride of lime was a popular disinfectant. Spirits of Salt (more commonly known now as hydrochloric acid) was a strong acid used to remove rust stains but which could damage fabrics. Lemon salts (or salts of lemon), better known now as citric acid, is a powerful drain cleaner and limescale remover. Finally, muriatic acid, a combination of hydrochloric acid and water, was used for cleaning cloudy glass.

The most effective cleaners you will ever need in the home today would therefore have been entirely recognisable to Mrs Praga: distilled vinegar, washing soda (soda crystals), bicarbonate of soda, borax (or borax substitute

TIP!

DON'T THROW AWAY YOUR OLD NEWSPAPERS: scrumpled newspaper is better than any cloth for cleaning windows.

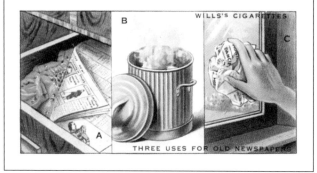

if you live in the European Union) and citric acid. If you can lay your hands on some long bars of green 'Fairy' soap (still available) it is a remarkably efficient grease remover.

2

Dust

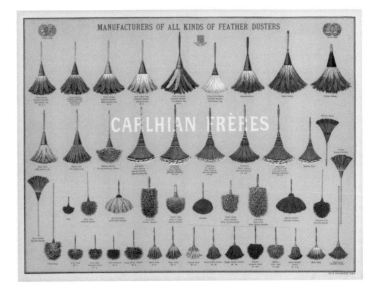

Rag mats shaken till the dust flew
Winifred Foley

T HERE IS ABSOLUTELY NO ESCAPING the universal presence that is dust. The moment dust is wiped away, back it comes, settling in a film over every available surface. Dust is composed of all the detritus of life: minuscule flakes of dead skin, hair and fur, the dried and finished top layer of organic matter that is constantly renewing itself. Dust is stirred up by harvest, by animals, vehicles, footfalls and wind.

A century ago, when horses were commoner than cars, several fires burned in every house and factory chimneys sent soot and smuts into the atmosphere, dust was thicker and more visible in everyday life. Rooms had to be swept out every day, curtains shaken, hats and coats brushed thoroughly after they had been worn outside. 'Dust and lay all smooth', was the first instruction of the day in William Kitchiner's *Housekeepers Oracle* of 1829. The battle against dust often seemed to represent a battle against outside life itself.

Carpets and Rugs

These were the most dust-collecting items in the house – and before the advent of vacuum cleaners they needed daily sweeping with a hard brush, or beating with a special-shaped beater as shown, in the open air. Damp tea-leaves or bicarbonate of soda were sprinkled over them to catch the dust and remove the smell of cigarette smoke, then swept up when dry. Winifred Foley, a housemaid in the 1920s, then went over rugs with water and deodorising vinegar to restore the faded colour. The 1850 *Finchley Guide to Home Economics in Industrial Schools* (the purpose of which was to teach young girls how to be domestic servants) suggested sponging grated potato on grease spots.

In nineteenth-century London, clouds of dust were in part the product of a new city rising, and the continual digging of foundations and excavations, and in part the product of an increasing population and its refuse and detritus. Thousands of tons of household dust, cinder-dust and ashes and the burned leavings of the city's kitchens, dust-holes and bins, were collected by dust contractors and transported to the suburbs where white mountains of the stuff accumulated, added to each day. The cinder-ash would be used mainly for making bricks that in turn were used to build the houses that were expanding London at such a rate. As Henry Mayhew observed of dust, 'there was considerable wealth in it'.

The Victorian middle-class home was in a constant fug of drawn curtains and hot fires, the dusty outside world kept at bay for the sake of health and cleanliness. Blinds were kept permanently down and curtains drawn to prevent the dirt of outdoors entering the home – and this especially guarded against sunlight with its swirling dust motes. In larger houses whole wings spent much of the year swathed in dustsheets. The bottom hems of curtains were bagged and coarsely woven protective sheets known as druggets were laid over carpets; glass lighting fitments were wrapped in muslin.

But the battle against dust has no winners. Constant daily dusting has very little effect on the problem, just moves it around from surface to surface. In 1907, the French doctor, Hericourt, observed: 'Dry sweeping and

OSTRICH FEATHER DUSTER: An expensive import from South Africa, ostrich feathers have little barbules on them that pick up dust particularly efficiently.

dusting are homicidal practices: they consist of taking dust which has been lying on the floor and on the furniture, mixing it in the atmosphere, and causing it to be swallowed and inhaled by the inhabitants of the house. In reality, it would be preferable to leave the dust alone where it is.'

BULLOCK's GALL was widely used in cleaning for centuries for removing impurities from textiles and wool. Carpets were scoured with the mixture, using a hard brush, then laboriously dried with cloths, every inch, so that the solution was not left on the rug.

In most modern cities, dust does not whip up quite the storm it once did. Horses and carts no longer bring in dust-coated animals and sacks of grain from the countryside. Coal and wood fires are rare, tarmac roads and pavements keep the earth from emerging between the cracks of cobbles or rough paths. The chief challenge posed by dust now lies mainly in its tendency to settle in places inaccessible even to a vacuum cleaner. Mrs Praga's suggestion that walls might be cleaned with a damp duster tied over a broom head is therefore still a useful one.

It seems surprising, given the prevalence of dust, that the Victorians were so enamoured of dust-collecting

> ## TIP!
>
> The damp-duster method remains the best. It's on the whole unnecessary to use anything but water (and not much of that) in dusting. Soak your duster and wring it as dry as you can. If you're going over wooden surfaces then make sure you dry them as you go along.

swags, pelmets, fringes and bric-a-brac. By the 1920s, advice manuals were urging readers to jettison clutter for streamlined furniture. Randal Phillips, author of *The Servantless House*, advocated the elimination of dust-trapping ridges and corners such as those on picture rails, dados and skirting by replacing these with round edges and furniture of tubular steel. Extravagant decorative details were out because they so easily became 'dust nests'. In Phillips's modernist ideal home, which displayed early counterparts of our own fitted kitchens and bathrooms, surfaces are smooth, made of industrial materials such as chrome, enamel and steel, and are easy to wipe clean.

This new aesthetic also raised the bar in the definition of clean: the home as a shining, dust-free laboratory was a vision promoted by the manufacturers of new cleaners

---

TIP!

BREAD: This unlikely cleaning method went with the usual old-fashioned thrifty idea of not throwing anything away until its last morsel had been exploited. Bread was used extensively in cleaning – and processed white bread, the kind that had become the cheap but un-nutritious staple of the diet of the poor – worked best of all. Pressing pieces of sliced white bread, screwed into pudgy balls, into the crevices of picture frames or dusty skirting boards picks up deposits of dust that can't be got at with dusters, fingers or feathers. Bread was also used for cleaning books: pressing a wodge of bread into the spine and cover of a book then wiping over with a very slightly damp cloth was recommended.

---

like Pledge as an achievable dream. Although advertisers and magazines promoted the idea that 'fifty percent of the time spent dusting has been reduced by wax polishes' (*Popular Science Monthly*, 1930), women were encouraged to believe that the modernist home would be less labour intensive found that in many regards its angles and surfaces promoted new pressures to achieve hospital levels of sanitation and tidiness.

> DUST MITE: No one has yet come up with a method of eradicating the miniscule dust mite – to be found wherever there is dust. Fortunately we don't have to look at dust mites: they are invisible to the human eye. The average home is crawling with millions of them.

In the eighteenth century, the Swedish traveller Per Kalm had noted that the stone and tile flags of English houses were particularly clean and a great deal of effort was put into keeping them scrubbed and dust free. But from the mid-nineteenth century the race was on to invent easy-wipe surfaces. In 1912, Formica, made from resin and paper, was invented and quickly became the

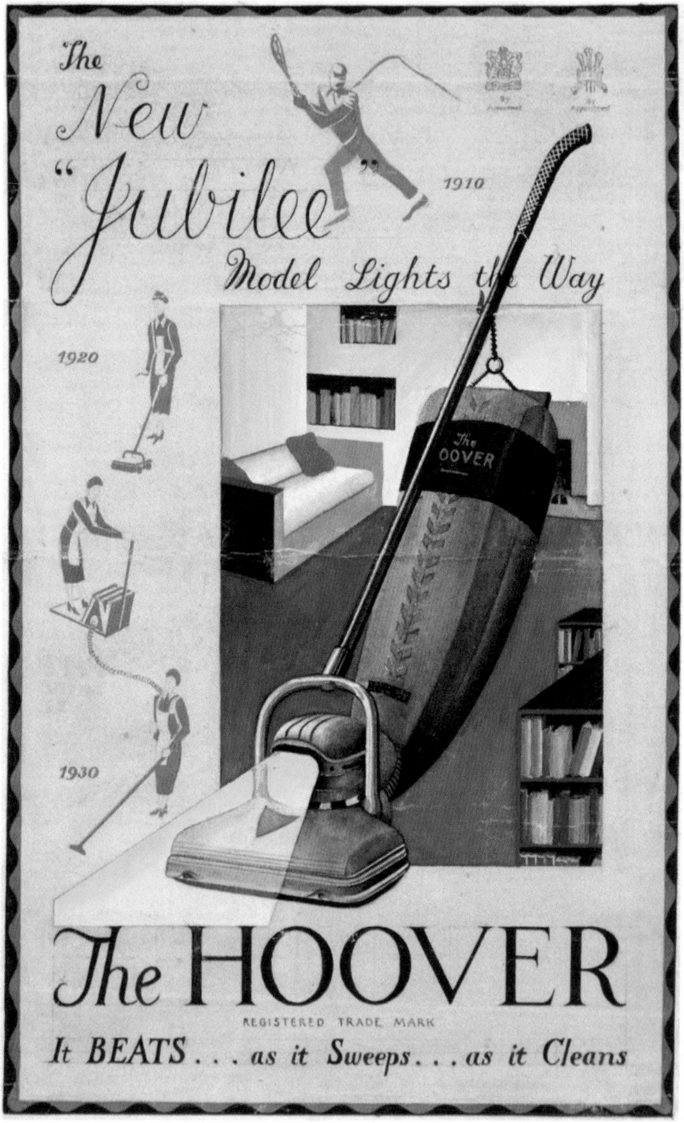
The
New
"Jubilee"
Model Lights the Way
1910
1920
1930
The HOOVER
The HOOVER
REGISTERED TRADE MARK
It BEATS . . . as it Sweeps . . . as it Cleans

most popular surface of choice in kitchens. And from its first creation in 1855, linoleum, made from solidified linseed oil combined with wood or cork dust, grew rapidly in popularity in Britain. Its wipe-easy surface meant that dust and dirt could be banished by a single swish with a damp mop. 'Time was when we holystoned and sanded fine patterns all over our stone floors,' wrote Dorothy Hartley in the 1930s, 'now we have fallen for linoleum.'

As Randal Phillips rightly pointed out, 'the only satisfactory way to deal with dust is to remove it altogether by collecting it in a sealed bag which can be taken away and emptied in the dust bin'. The invention of the vacuum cleaner therefore was arguably the most important technological advance in domestic cleaning. The vacuum cleaner revolutionised the relationship of a domestic interior with the dusty outside world: now dust particles could be sucked up in a matter of minutes.

It took some time for the vacuum, invented in the late nineteenth century, to be manufactured in models that were small and reasonably priced enough for domestic use. Manufacturers capitalised on lingering concerns among middle-class housewives that the status conferred by having servants was threatened by new technology – and they gave the first portable vacuum cleaners names such as 'Mary Ann' and 'Daisy' that suggested they might be considered as a mechanical maid.

3

Laundry

A firmament of drying clothes
Flora Thompson

T HE TWO MOST IMPORTANT INGREDIENTS required for washing fabrics are water and constant agitation. For thousands of years, woven materials of all kinds have been pummelled, beaten and pulled about under running water. Scrubbing or pounding opens up the weave of a material so that dirt can be more easily be removed. The modern electric washing machine simply reproduces the motion of slinging fabric against rocks on a riverbank. It was common practice in Scotland, well into the nineteenth century, to trample the washing wearing wooden clogs. (And if you have the energy for it, the barefoot method is still an effective way to wash a down duvet in a bathtub.)

Over the centuries, ingenious technologies attempted to mimic the action of churning and beating. The beetle was one of the oldest, a corrugated wooden bat which beat clothes against a hard surface. Garments submerged in troughs of water were manipulated by log-shaped 'possers' which stamped on them. Then there were dolleys, three-legged devices on a pole inside a wooden

BRUSHING is the best method of cleaning outdoor clothes in tweed, wool or cloth. It is still almost always unnecessary to get coats and jackets commercially dry-cleaned. The brushing room in a large country house was in the servants' quarters. It was a spartan utility room with shelves or racks along one side and a large brushing table in the middle. There were varieties of specialist clothes brushes on offer: heavy-duty tweed, for example, was brushed by a dandy brush with long bristles made of straw. But good brushing requires only a natural bristle brush and the appliance of strong sweeping strokes in the same direction. Valets used a dry clothes brush to loosen caked-on dirt, then a very slightly damp one to freshen up the cloth. It works a treat and really does help preserve good wools and tweeds.

barrel or corrugated 'peggy tub'. In the early nineteenth century, washing machines were wooden tubs rocked or rotated by hand. The washboard, with its ridges and ribs, was designed to imitate the knobbly power of the human knuckle rubbing and pounding the dirt out of textiles.

The work of washing clothes has been relieved by modern technology more than almost any other domestic labour. Before the domestic proliferation of

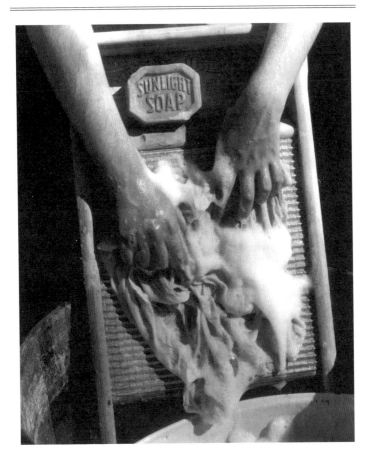

first the mangle and then, between the wars, the washing machine, the weekly washday was time-consuming and laborious. Dorothy Hartley, in the 1930s, noted: 'The older washing processes were divided into steeping, bucking [*see* p. 39], boiling and scouring (before you got

37

to pressing, ironing and finishing), and they all had complicated sub-divisions.'

Laundry was the single most exhausting and labour-intensive domestic occupation of the house. The large country estates had outhouses which functioned entirely as laundries and drying rooms, often employing the latest steam-driven equipment and staffed by a team of laundry maids. But in more modest houses, most of the work took place outside, as the processes required so much space. In late-nineteenth-century Oxfordshire, Flora Thompson remembered the awful discomfort of a winter washday in a cottage with only clothes horses to hang washing on. 'No-one who has not experienced it can imagine the misery of living for several days with a firmament of drying clothes on lines overhead.'

Clothes and household linen first had to be sorted, then they were scrubbed of surface dirt with a bristle brush (paying particular attention to cuffs and collars) on a wooden work table and some all-purpose soap such as Sunlight or carbolic, before they were placed in a dolley or a tub and washboard with soap suds and boiling water carried from the copper. They were swirled and churned by hand for about an hour before being put through a mangle to remove as much of the soapy water as possible. Then came the rinsing process: using several tin tubs of cold, clean water, carried from a pump or tap, and yet more agitation, until the washing was thoroughly soap free. Finally the garments were taken out of the water, put yet again through a mangle, and hung up to dry.

W. H. Lever had begun selling all-purpose Sunlight laundry soap in 1884, in packages of two square tablets stamped with the word 'Sunlight'. But it was the invention of flakes that took the labour out of creating laundry soap – an arduous business that had involved grating pieces of hard soap into boiling water, then

LYE, sometimes known as potash or caustic soda, has been the most important ingredient of soap since antiquity. Lye, an alkali, when combined with fat goes through a saponification process, creating suds and becoming soluble. Lye used to be made by passing water through wood ash, dried ferns or burned seaweed but since the nineteenth century has been generally made from mineral salts – and is far more powerful as a result (neat caustic soda is a violently aggressive drain cleaner). Before the advent of manufactured soap, most people made their own, using balls of potash lye combined with scraps of household fat – fish oils and slaughter refuse particularly. Sometimes lye was applied neat – a method known as bucking that removed the most virulent stains before the boiling wash.

whipping it up into a lather. This process was hard on hands and laundry maids disliked it intensely. Sunlight and Lux were marketed with adjectives like 'gentle', stressing how sensitive skin could be protected by flakes and powders.

The key to a good laundry is soft water. 'The softest, and I believe by far the best, water for hand washing is country rainwater that's has been strained through gauze or fine linen,' wrote Stanley Ager. 'Because rainwater is so soft it brings up a wonderful lather when detergent is used with it.' Soft water means you need to use less soap – which is why collecting rainwater to use for laundering was recommended during the Second World War when soap was rationed. But because the business of collecting rainwater is a faff in any age, and unpredictable to boot, there are many shortcut methods to softening water that take a matter of seconds. Adding a tablespoonful of borax or washing soda to powdered detergent helps and so does putting a cupful of white vinegar in your final rinse.

If the linens were white, this final rinse might once have contained a muslin bag of 'blue', the popular additive made of French ultramarine (and still used in many

SOAPWORT: The roots of the Soapwort plant (sometimes known as latherwort) are rich in saponins that clean and dissolve grease. Its Latin name is *saponaria*. The leaves and stems of a flowering soapwort, boiled in water, or bruised leaves soaked overnight, produce a liquid particularly good for washing fragile textiles.

modern laundry detergents) that gave white clothes a blue/white dazzle and prevented the yellowing that was a by-product of soap made with tallow. Cream dolly bags

took the grey out of net curtains. White was the colour of cleanliness, purity, sterilisation and innocence, the colour of choice for bath towels, bed-linen, nightdresses and children's clothes.

Stains

INK: Press a teaspoon of citric acid onto the spots (using a bone spoon) and moisten with water. Then pour boiling water over the stains until they disappear.

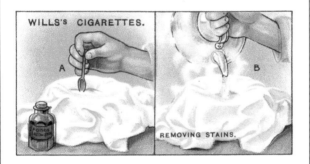

WINE OR FRUIT: Stretch the fabric over a bowl and pour boiling water through it until the stain disappears.

RUST: Stewed rhubarb, spread over the stain, left for a few hours and washed off, is pretty effective. (Boiled fig leaves work just as well.) *See also* p. 55.

BLOOD: soak thoroughly in cold, salty water for an hour or so before washing.

OLD COFFEE OR TEA STAINS: can be soaked in a diluted solution of methylated spirits, half a cup to two cups of water. Leave garments to soak for an hour, then wash as normal.

SCORCH MARKS: Bruise 2 onions then boil in half a pint of vinegar with some grated soap and two ounces of Fuller's Earth. When cooled, apply mixture to scorch mark and rinse off when dry.

MILDEW: soak for a few hours in buttermilk before washing.

There are innumerable methods of bleaching white materials. Before ammonia was available in neat form, the ammonia in human urine or cow dung was used for the job. Many bleaching methods, however, leave fabrics falling to bits. Mrs Praga warned her readers to avoid cheap laundresses who used strong chemicals.

Borax is a gentler whitening alternative. 'There is nothing like borax for whitening clothes and it does not rot the linen,' advised *The Ladies Treasury* of 1872. A prewash soak in a solution of borax will brighten greying fabrics. Kitchen maids tasked with washing tea towels often rubbed raw potato on the cloths before boiling them, repeating the process, then steeping for an hour in cold water before rinsing.

Sunlight is the best bleach. Large houses once had bleaching lawns on which large sheets and towels were laid to dry. Winter, or indirect, sunlight is more effective than bright summer sun, which yellows fabric, and so the lawns were never in exposed parts of the garden.

After the drying came the starching process. Starch was required for linen and cotton – particularly men's shirts, children's clothes and aprons and petticoats that were meant to be smooth and structured. Powdered

starch, made from wheat bran or rice, was commercially produced and could be dissolved in boiling water. The clothes were submerged, then squeezed dry and ironed to stiffness while still slightly damp. It was recommended that delicate lace be soaked in the liquid in which some white rice had been boiled.

The final labour was ironing. Irons were heated over a fire or stove and then pressed onto dry linen. Intricate articles such as lace or ribbons were 'goffered', wrapped around a hot goffering iron. This would take hours and

TIP!

HANG SUITS OR COATS OVER THE BATH where the steam will freshen them up and remove any lingering smells of cigarette smoke.

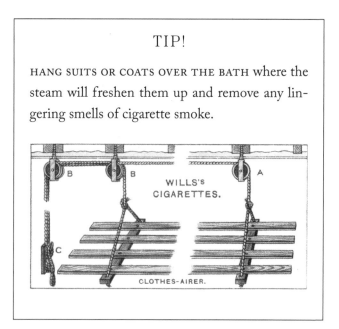

WILLS'S CIGARETTES.

CLOTHES-AIRER.

the heat made laundresses' hands hard as boards. Steam was sometimes applied – the same principle we use today with electric steam irons.

And then the washing was finally over – for another week.

Sunlight Soap

The first branded form of laundry soap flakes, Lever Bros. Sunlight Flakes, was launched in 1899, then renamed Lux in 1900.

4

The Kitchen Sink

Immersed in greasy water
Margaret Powell

T HE LABOUR OF WASHING DISHES has been substan-
tially reduced now that most people no longer go
in for the kind of gargantuan meals that punctuated life
in a pre-war country house. 'When there were visitors,
[there were] four different kinds of eggs and bacon, saus-
ages, kidneys and always a kedgeree, cold ham and cold
tongue and scones with butter and Devonshire cream,'
wrote Helen Mildmay-White about the breakfasts she
remembered in the 1930s. These were followed by four-
course lunches, teas with cake (fresh every day) and bread
and butter, then dinner of several courses. Family meals
were only one part of the picture as servants needed
feeding too. In 1900 researcher Arthur Ponsonby found
one wealthy young man living in London with fourteen
servants. He had 300 eggs sent up from his country es-
tate every week by train, as well as fruit, vegetables and
poultry. Still, Ponsonby's report noted: 'Quarts of cream
are emptied down the sink, joints and birds only half

eaten are thrown away, and the pig tub received a rich enough allowance of vegetables, fruit and cake to satisfy the appetites of a rich family.'

Despite, by the end of the nineteenth century, the popularity of cheap tinned foodstuffs such as pineapple and

Copper Pans

Before the Second World War, the most visible indication of the *batterie de cuisine* of a large kitchen was a gleaming array of copper pans. Copper is ideal for cooking because of its high conductivity of heat – but it is a chore to clean. It will scratch and tarnish if scoured too roughly in too much sloshing water. For kitchen-maids, silversand (a very fine silica sand now chiefly used as topsoil in gardening) was a common ingredient for cleaning copper, mixed with malt vinegar or lemon and then rubbed into the pan. Edna Wheway cleaned fifty copper pans a week with green carbolic soap. She followed this with a paste of whitening powder (a fine chalk powder) mixed with vegetable oil and then rubbed in with a cloth, rinsed off and dried thoroughly. Lemons make an easy and effective copper cleaner: just take the shells of squeezed lemons and dip them in cooking salt. Then gently scrub the copper saucepan with them, rinse and dry well, and polish to a shine.

salmon, and the introduction of American breakfast cereals in the 1920s, most meals, in all homes from rich to poor, were still made from scratch. Much of a family's status rested on the display of a dinner party. Each course – soup, savoury, meat, fish, pudding – required different china, an array of glasses and numerous pieces of cutlery. No wonder Arnold Bennett's fictional maid Elsie, housemaid to a socially ambitious London couple in his story *Elsie and the Child*, called their dinner tables 'like a church'.

Culinary tastes shifted when there were no longer as many people available to help with the washing up. In his 1928 book *How To Plan Your Home*, Martin Briggs advised that the 'bogy of washing up' was 'more likely to be dispelled by increased simplicity in the nature of our meals than by any mechanical invention applicable to the needs of small homes'. It was the beginning of the end for the daily cooked breakfast, the freshly baked cake for afternoon tea and those extravagantly fiddly, decorative dishes that had once been so fashionable. By the mid-twentieth century, even grander houses began to accommodate the idea of shop-bought marmalade.

Nonetheless, the average meal fifty years ago still used a large array of apparatus. With the cooking utensils closely followed by the eating utensils, washing up was an almost continual labour for kitchen-maids. No sooner was one

TIP!

STAINED ENAMEL PANS: Stains on enamel pans can be removed by stewed rhubarb (*see* p. 43). If you don't want to eat the rhubarb, just use a single stick with its leaves still on and simmer for ten minutes. Leave the mixture in the pan for an hour or so – the result will be pristine enamel. Stewed figs or sorrel work just as well.

Boiling water in a stained pan with a little borax or washing soda in it will also help lift hardened dirt – as will soaking a pan in the same solution overnight.

set of pans and dishes washed than it was time to heat the water and prepare to deal with the next load. Mrs Emmitt, a kitchen maid in the 1920s, remembered that the worst grind of food preparation lay in the constant puréeing. 'It was really slavery because you had a beautiful kitchen, three huge ovens to cook with but the work that was entailed in putting spinach through very fine hair sieves…' These sieves were a particular horror to clean: minute morsels got trapped between the hairs and the sieves had to be washed, rinsed and washed again, all in cold water because the food scraps would cook in hot.

Before the widespread use of stainless steel cutlery (a steel alloy with a chromium addition which prevented rusting) and in 1938 the breakthrough invention of non-stick Teflon, washing up was a continual battle against rust and corrosion on the one hand and hardened, burnt-on foodstuffs on the other. Metals had to be dried instantly to avoid rust and knives were rubbed with mutton fat, rolled in brown paper and stored in a dry place after every out-

Bath Brick

Bath brick, a hard scouring pad made from west country clay and patented in 1823, was a widely popular choice of material for cleaning knives. When the stone was wetted the knives were polished directly on to it.

ing. Knife cleaning was the work of the hall boy or 'boots', the lowest rung of male domestic service. Anne Cobbett, author of an 1835 manual for domestic servants, maintained that it was 'next to impossible' for a woman to clean knives properly: 'it is an essentially masculine occupation'.

Mrs Beeton was also of the opinion that specialist washing up should be left to men, particularly glass, which

---

TIP!

TARNISHED SILVER: Never put silver or plate in the dishwasher. To remove tarnish, line a washing-up bowl with aluminium foil, place the cutlery on top, pour on a cup of washing soda (or baking soda) and enough very hot water to cover the contents. When the water stops bubbling and hissing, the silver will be ready to take out and hand wash as usual, then polish. *See also* p. 69.

'requires great care in washing'. Her advice was always to wash glass in hot water and rinse in cold, and to add a cup of vinegar to the final rinse to bring up the shine.

It was only during the Second World War that writer Lesley Lewis discovered how arduous washing up had been for her pre-war kitchen-maids: 'I realised how inconvenient the equipment was. Possibly the sinks had not been too low in the days when most people were shorter, but the width across them to the taps was singularly ill-adapted to any human frame.'

The widespread use of bicarbonate of soda (made into a paste with water) as a scourer fell into disuse with the widespread popularity of aluminium saucepans, as bicarb attacks the aluminium's protective oxide layer. But modern washing-up detergent, created during the First World

War when there was a shortage of the fats and oils required to make soap bars, is a descendant of the traditional combination of softening washing soda and grated soap.

As for washing implements: in Stanley Ager's view, the softness and resilience of the sea sponge is unbeatable for cleaning porcelain. For washing up, as for so many household chores, the labour-intensive was generally favoured over the labour-saving device. In Dorset in the 1920s, kitchen-maid Edna Wheway's employer returned from a holiday in Jamaica bearing the husk of a coconut which she suggested would make an ideal scrubbing brush. And for many there was nothing as effective as bare fingers for digging deep inside the crevices of a

---

TIP!

TO FRESHEN A THERMOS put crushed eggshells in it and fill with vinegar. Leave it to stand for a few hours then empty, rinse and dry thoroughly.

SINKS were traditionally made of earthenware, metal or ceramic – though these hard surfaces risked washing-up breakages. This led to the brief popularity of teak sinks which minimised the risk of shattering china.

jelly mould. No wonder hot water and washing soda left kitchen-maids' hands red and raw. Mutton fat, smeared on at night then covered with gloves, was one solution; so was an ointment called glymiel jelly, used by Edna Wheway. 'When the corners of each thumb split and bled, I went to the chemist for advice. I was so ashamed of my hands that I waited until no-one else was in the shop.'

Rubber gloves did not come into general use until after the Second World War – and they must rate as one of the more life-changing of all domestic innovations.

DISHWASHERS: Early dishwashers were not always satisfactory; washing up dishes proved a harder challenge for technological innovation than washing clothes. Their increasing popularity inspired a report from the Master Silversmiths' Association in the 1930s which attributed some stains on silver to the use of new powdered detergents. Randal Phillips, that early champion of new household technologies, gave muted approval to the 'Polliwashup', a 1920s innovation which nonetheless still required the operator to boil water and make a lather with grated soap, then crank a handle six times in each direction. Easier, but messier, was another early design which involved stacking the dirty dishes in a specially designed tray and firing a jet of hot water at them from a rubber hose.

5

Bringing Up a Shine

Polishing a chandelier is like milking a cow
Stanley Ager

T HE SHININESS OF CERTAIN DOMESTIC objects held a particular appeal when homes were lit only by candlelight. Gleaming brass, copper, silver and the deep patinas of old wood glow richly in half-light. A display of shining metal, of pewter, silver or gold, was an indication of wealth and status, a legacy, observed the Victorian architect Robert Kerr, of the medieval hall where 'on the tables and buffet of the dais, the wealth of a king or a great courtier was daily displayed in a collection of gold and silver plate'. Front door brass furniture in all its inviting pomp was the Victorian urban equivalent of medieval swank.

A deep polish feeds natural materials: leather and wood needs regular nourishment to bring out their grain (nineteenth-century household manuals often refer to wax polishing as 'warming the wood') and metals will get tarnished and dull if they are not rubbed and fed. Even utilitarian objects like the stove used to be polished

> ## TIP!
>
> HOMEMADE POLISH: Melt two ounces of beeswax
> (it comes in blocks or sticks) over a bowl of boil-
> ing water, adding two dessertspoons of turpentine.
> Blend these together well (with care because it is
> highly flammable) with a tablespoon of wine vin-
> egar. Continue heating and blending till you have
> a smooth consistency, then pour the mixture into a
> large jar. Cool, then seal with parchment.

with black-lead every day. Dorothy Hartley, travelling in Lancashire, found that the county 'shines in black-lead'. Hartley was amazed at how gleaming a stove could become with some elbow grease: 'Give an ex-mill lass a pennyworth of black-lead in a gallypot with mysterious vinegar and beeswax and she'll produce a gleaming miracle of black satin.'

For old-fashioned servants, polishing was an art that required time and practice. Shoes, left outside the bedroom door every night in grander houses, were shined each day. The high gleam on popular patent leather for example was enhanced by the application of milk (or sometimes Vaseline). Leather shoes last for decades when properly polished. Dubbin, a waxy substance made chiefly of tallow, had been used to maintain leather since

TIP!

REMOVING SEA-WATER STAINS FROM LEATHER SHOES: Dissolve a teaspoon of washing soda in two tablespoonfuls of hot milk. Apply to the stain on a cloth and wait for it to dry. Repeat, then polish with a wax shoe polish.

REMOVING SEA-WATER STAINS FROM BROWN SHOES

medieval times – but when shiny shoes came into fashion in the nineteenth century, beeswax polishes became more popular as they buffed up a higher shine.

Servants (specifically footmen or butlers) spent an inordinate amount of time cleaning silver and plate. It was very hard, physical, intensive work. Footmen's hands were 'hard as boards', remembered Ernest King, a butler between the wars. 'Cleaning plate is hell. It's the greatest bugbear behind the green baize door, the hardest job in the house. When I began this work, rubbing the silver,

> ## TIP!
>
> GILT: Freshen up the colour and shine of gilt picture frames by going over them with a soft brush dipped in water in which three or four onions have been boiled for an hour.

the spoons and the forks, occasionally getting a prong in my thumb, my fingers grew fearfully sore and blistered, but in those days if you complained you were just told to get on with it and you did. The blisters burst and you kept on despite the pain and you developed a pair of plate hands that never blistered again.'

Rubbing hard with fingers and thumbs generated heat more effectively than a cloth, and allowed the polish to impregnate the metal, giving it a blueish tinge. 'In the old days', remembered butler Peter Russell, 'you could tell an under-butler by the state of the balls of his thumbs.' A toothbrush can be used to get the paste deep into the crevices of embossed silver.

Glass, mirrors and chandeliers refracted candlelight and needed to be polished to a high shine. A servants' manual of 1850 suggested using gin and water for cleaning mirrors, applied with a clean silk handkerchief. Butler Stanley Ager recommended annual washing of chandeliers with hot water mixed with a mild deter-

SILVER: The care of silver and silver plate is a battle against tarnish. Silver tarnishes because of exposure to oxygen – which is why silver tableware is traditionally wrapped tightly in brown paper then stored in green felt to keep it out of the air. But foodstuffs containing sulphur also cause tarnish: these include asparagus, onions, cabbage, garlic, rhubarb, grouse and broccoli; the sulphur in eggs makes silver go blue. Hairspray, rubber bands, wool and many cosmetic lotions will have the same effect on silver jewellery. Polishing silver really well is a science and an art. In the 1830s, Joseph Goddard cornered the silver-polish market with a silver powder which added to water made a pink paste.

For the old-fashioned silver polisher, only a real animal skin should be considered for the final buffing up – a fake chamois leather is an affront to a craftsman.

gent and a cup of vinegar. The glass droplets were then rubbed dry with a clean cloth, one by one. The work, Ager found, was 'rather like milking a cow. It has the same rhythmic movement – you wipe, you polish, you wipe you polish.' Marble, its cool surfaces popular in bathrooms and kitchens, as well as for light-fittings, was cleaned with lemon juice then rubbed with a little vegetable oil to bring up the lustre.

Randal Phillips, in the 1920s, pointed out that in most homes an inconvenient amount of the day was spent on this daily labour of keeping things shiny. There is a great deal to remember about how best to look after different woods and metals. Pewter, for example, should never be polished with metal polish but with whiting. Although most oils (even food oils such as olive and vegetable, though they smell a bit rank) are good for polishing, a really good beeswax mixture is still the best possible nourishment for wood. And it had to be made from scratch. There were multiple variants on the recipe: housemaid Winifred Foley recalled making her own furniture polish in the 1920s by boiling up a 'mixture of beeswax, vinegar and linseed oil'. Wooden floors were mopped with a mixture

TIP!

REMOVING WATER STAINS FROM POLISHED FURNITURE: Put kitchen salt on the stain, then dab on a little methylated spirits and rub briskly. Then polish *immediately* with beeswax polish on a second cloth. It is important not to let the meths sit on the stain for too long.

REMOVING STAINS FROM POLISHED FURNITURE

of beeswax and turpentine. Foley wrote: 'The beeswax had to be soaked in turpentine in jars the night before, then it melted and you had a stick and put it on the rag – all the floors were done with beeswax – all on the knees.'

Care also went into looking after the equipment: polishing cloths (the ones used for taking off polish), for example, were always ironed – not because in the past they had an excessive concern for a display of neatness but because a smooth cloth does a better job. Scraps of

---

TIP!

CANDLE WAX: Mrs Beeton suggested pouring boiling water over candlesticks to take off the old wax. Twelve hours in a freezer works too.

---

leftover velvet were often sewn into very effective buffing pads with old rags as stuffing. According to butler Stanley Ager, well-washed, well-worn women's underwear, the flimsier the better, was second to none when it came to buffing up a shine on wood and leather.

BONING: Leather shoes and boots were polished to a high shine. The task of cleaning the household's boots generally fell to the hallboy – on the lowest rung of the male servants' hierarchy – but hunting boots and proper leather shoes were in the care of the valet. The best polisher for leather boots was traditionally considered the foreleg of a deer, preferably a female, and the process of using it known as boning. Stanley Ager still had his own bone after he retired in 1975 (though he said that the leather on modern shoes was too thin to bear the friction): after all those years of polishing, 'The colour is so brilliant you'd think it was made of amber.' The foreleg, its edges smoothed by use, would be worked deep into the leather of a pair of hunting boots until the scratches were removed.

Above all, a good polish requires time, and Randal Phillips, the champion of low-maintenance housekeeping, had it in his sights when it came to efficient time management. He recommended that brass door knockers and letterboxes be painted over with black enamel paint to cut out the chore of early morning polishing. Phillips also advised that furniture in satiny woods like walnut and mahogany be replaced by limed or varnished oak that didn't need as much elbow grease, and he advocated surfaces that were deliberately dulled, bleached and rough-hewn. It was the end of the age of the high shine.

6

Pests

ECONOMIC DINING ESTABLISHMENT.

For even then cometh the enemy
The *Lady's Everyday Book* (1875)

I N 1770, *The Vermin-Killer (being a complete and necessary family-book)* listed the dismaying range of animal and insect horrors that intruded on the eighteenth-century householder, 'shewing a ready Way to destroy' them. Among them were 'Adders, Badgers, Birds of all Sorts, Earwigs, Caterpillars, Flies, Fish, Foxes, Frogs, Gnats, Mice, Otters, Pismires [ants], Pole-Cats, Rabbits, Norway and other Rats, Snakes, Scorpions, Snails, Spiders, Toads, Wasps Wasles, Wants or Moles, Worms in Houses and Gardens, Bugs, Lice, Fleas &c.' By and large, pests and vermin like dark, un-ventilated spaces, where things aren't moved around a lot. Eighteenth-century houses were inadequately aired, particularly rooms of 'sick and sweating people', the stale air of which *The Vermin-Killer* warns was particularly prone to incubating bugs of all kinds.

To the modern reader, it would seem almost preferable to endure an infestation than to attempt a cure.

Keatings Insect Powder

This claimed to be 'Unrivalled in destroying fleas, bugs, beetles, cockroaches and moths'.

The Vermin-Killer suggests that moles could be banished from the garden by taking 'garlick onion or leek and stop it in their holes – they'll run out amazed' and could be then merrily clubbed to death. As a deterrent to bed bugs *The Vermin-Killer* suggested washing the joints of your bedhead in wormwood boiled in urine, or burning brimstone under the bed, or daubing the bedroom with rabbits' guts boiled in water or a concoction of vinegar and ox gall. As a last resort you might even hang the skin of a freshly killed bear in your bedroom.

Most people would rather live with fleas than anoint themselves with badgers' blood to keep them at bay. Swinging a half-dead and shrieking rat about a room as a deterrent to other rats is even less appealing. Nonetheless, rats in the house are a horror. The attitude of Mrs Annie Butterworth, author of *The Manual of Household Work and Management* (1902) is typical of a hardier generation.

> ## TIP!
>
> COCKROACHES are particularly partial to cucumber.
> Leave strips of cucumber on the floor of the kitchen
> at night and it will send them into a stupor which
> makes them easier to stamp on in the morning.

Observing that 'vigorous thumping and squeaking in the wainscots are often the sign of rats', she recommends shoving rags saturated with carbolic acid into the rats' holes as it will not only finish them off but dissolve their flesh and avoid the smell of a decomposing corpse.

The poorest houses, particularly in the urban slums, were most afflicted by vermin. One missionary reported entering a slum tenement and finding 'the quantity of vermin is amazing... I have felt them dropping on my hat from the ceiling like peas.' Wealthier houses, however, were not immune. The memories of kitchen-maids are full of kitchens plagued by black beetles, ants and cockroaches. 'I found black beetles all over the floor so I cleared off,' wrote Dolly Davey in the 1920s. Kitchen servants customarily left traps in the form of bowls of sugar and water over the kitchen floor – the pests drowned when they fell in. Food had to be covered always (those little muslin covers with beaded edges made

INSECTICIDES: Among the most popular insecticides, used on flies, bed bugs, fleas and garden pests, was one of the oldest and it is still in production today: Persian Powder. Made from the powdered roots and leaves of plants in the chrysanthemum family, Persian Powder can be sprinkled over mattresses to kill bed bugs or added to water to spray flies. In 1924, Harold Lefroy, a professor of entomology, patented a spray that would destroy the deadly wood-worm. He called it Ento-Kill and its success led to Lefroy forming a company known today as Rentokil.

by ladies for bazaars were for this purpose) as a roaring infestation of ants or beetles could appear almost over-night. Long, sticky fly-papers, studded with black bodies, customarily festooned the working areas of a large house. Wooden skirting and bedsteads were scrubbed regularly with carbolic to deter insects from laying eggs in cracks. Onion water (*see also* p. 68), brushed over picture frames and other surfaces was thought a good way of deterring flies and their eggs, although *The Vermin-Killer* suggested they'd be driven mad by the scent of burning hens' feath-ers waved in their direction.

Flesh-eating bed bugs, and their itchy bites, were familiar to all classes. Few households were free of them. An infected room was said to smell of rotting raspberries.

When Beatrix Potter stayed at the Osborne Hotel in Torquay in 1893, she wrote in her diary: 'I sniffed my bedroom on arrival and for a few hours felt a certain grim satisfaction when my forebodings were maintained. But it is possible to have too much natural history in a bed.'

Carpet beetles were a particularly virulent menace in the days before furnishings in artificial fibres. The larvae of the

---

TIP!

BEDBUGS: Make sure your bed is not squeezed too tight against the wall. Allow a gap in order that air can circulate about the bed.

> ## TIP!
>
> CARPET MOTHS: Dissolve 25 ml of ammonia in a bucket filled with boiling water and place a cloth in the bucket. Wring as much liquid out as possible and lay it on the carpet. Then iron over the cloth with a hot iron. Repeat all over the carpet.
>
>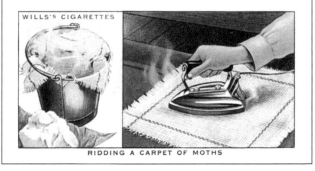
>
> RIDDING A CARPET OF MOTHS

carpet beetle, known as 'woolly bear' are often even more lethal than moths. They are ravenous, feeding mainly on textiles, particularly wool, but also on other animal-based materials such as horn, tortoiseshell, and stuffed birds and animals. Like moths, carpet beetles fly blithely into the house through open windows in the autumn and lay their eggs on anything undisturbed – carpets, rugs and dead flies. They absolutely adore pet hair and piles of lint. An infestation of carpet beetles is a good reason occasionally to give the house a spring clean. The best way to get rid

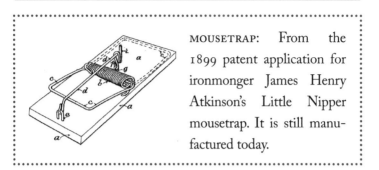

MOUSETRAP: From the 1899 patent application for ironmonger James Henry Atkinson's Little Nipper mousetrap. It is still manufactured today.

of them is vigilant vacuuming in every corner of the carpets and upholstery – particularly the bottoms of curtains, where they often lurk undetected.

There are innumerable recommendations for poisons and deterrents to keep pests at bay. A sprinkling of cloves or oil of cloves, for instance, was thought to keep red ants out of the kitchen. The dried leaves of the bog myrtle, which have antibacterial qualities, made an excellent midge repellent. Once mice are nesting in the house it's difficult to remove them but rural households swore by the leaves of the elderberry, the laurel or the rose. If you stopped a mouse hole with any of these, or strewed them about the house, mice were expected to give up and go elsewhere.

Moths in particular are thought to be deterred by strong odours – although our ancestors struggled as vainly as we do now to keep them out of the wardrobe. 'For even then cometh the enemy', wrote the anonymous author of the *Lady's Everyday Book* despairingly.

If you succeeded in banishing the moth, the price paid for moth-hole free clothing was that it absolutely stank. It is hardly surprising that the fragrant (though not always particularly effective) alternatives of cedar wood, dried rose petals and lavender remained most popular. In 1892, *Enquire Within* suggested that lumps of brimstone (sulphur), although they had 'no odour perceivable', would be detected by moths that could 'very quickly recognize it'. Whether brimstone repellents took off, history does not relate.

TIP!

CLOTHES MOTHS: Once or twice a year, wipe the insides of drawers and wardrobes with ammonia to deter moths and prevent them both laying eggs and fertilising eggs already laid on clothing.

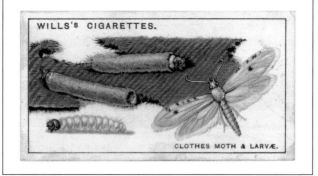

WILLS'S CIGARETTES.

CLOTHES MOTH & LARVÆ.

Most traditional methods of moth deterrent involve ingredients that smell absolutely disgusting. Taking up smoking might be a last resort: Stanley Ager observed that clothes worn by men who habitually smoked cigars were seldom troubled by moths. Other hard-hitting smells were camphor (the chief ingredient of mothballs), ground pepper, bay leaves, paraffin, cedar wood, leather, oil of cloves, caraway, ammonia and turpentine. A piece of tarred rope was said to keep moths out of fur.

Victorian chemists sold little muslin bags containing dried *Citrullus colocynthis*, small hard fruits also known as bitter apples (and sometimes as desert gourd) as a moth repellent.

Clothes were sealed in boxes every season to keep the moths out and households were advised to check lofts, attics and chimneys regularly for old birds' nests – as these are often the place where moth larvae infestations, both textile and carpet moths, originate.

7

The Water Closet

Tubbed, scrubbed, deodorised
Theodor Rosebury, bacteriologist

W E ARE LESS COMFORTABLE WITH SMELLS of decay, mould and human waste than our distant ancestors would have been, and we have found all sorts of means of concealing them. This attitude may have something to do with the miasmatic theory that was so prevalent in the first part of the nineteenth century – which held that disease was actually transmitted through smells. Many influential Victorian figures were convinced of it, including the reformers Edwin Chadwick ('All smell is disease') and Florence Nightingale who advocated that drains and sewers should not be laid beneath residential areas as odours might escape and infect the inhabitants with diseases such as smallpox and scarlet fever. Some scientists even briefly considered the possibility that 'emanations' from putrefying animal matter in sewers and graveyards created the 'miasma' that caused cholera.

From the 1870s, Pasteur's germ theory effectively put paid to this idea but nonetheless, the association

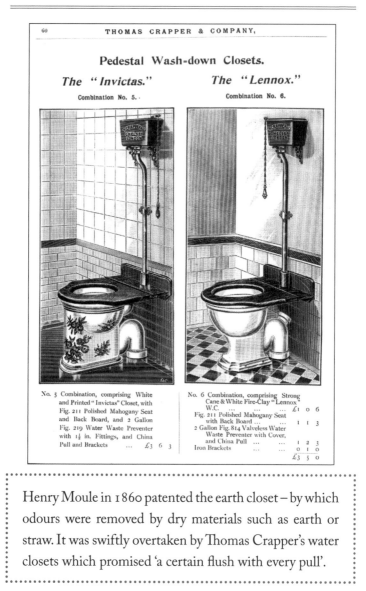

Pedestal Wash-down Closets.

The "Invictas."
Combination No. 5.

The "Lennox."
Combination No. 6.

No. 5 Combination, comprising White and Printed "Invictas" Closet, with Fig. 211 Polished Mahogany Seat and Back Board, and 2 Gallon Fig. 219 Water Waste Preventer with 1½ in. Fittings, and China Pull and Brackets ... £3 6 3

No. 6 Combination, comprising Strong Cane & White Fire-Clay "Lennox" W.C. £1 0 6
Fig. 211 Polished Mahogany Seat with Back Board ... 1 1 3
2 Gallon Fig. 814 Valveless Water Waste Preventer with Cover, and China Pull 1 2 3
Iron Brackets 0 1 0
£3 5 0

Henry Moule in 1860 patented the earth closet – by which odours were removed by dry materials such as earth or straw. It was swiftly overtaken by Thomas Crapper's water closets which promised 'a certain flush with every pull'.

of smells and uncleanliness remains well-founded. It is quite true that smells can be a warning of poor ventilation or sewage – which in turn can damage health. In 1900, Florence Stacpoole, a hygiene campaigner, pointed out: 'when you perceive a bad smell something unclean and perhaps poisonous touches you. It is a warning.' Mrs Stacpoole recommended checking that drains are clear by going to the highest lavatory in the house and pouring down it a bottle of peppermint oil followed by a jug of boiling water. If you can smell the peppermint in the drain outside then your drains are free of blockages.

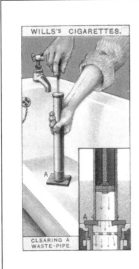

WILLS'S CIGARETTES.

CLEARING A
WASTE-PIPE.

TIP!

DRAINS: Keep your plug-holes clear of gunk by pouring into them a weekly tablespoonful of bicarbonate of soda, followed by a cup of white vinegar. When it has fizzed and spluttered for a minute or two, pour in a kettleful of boiling water.

Proponents of miasma theory ushered in an obsession with fresh air, with opening windows, and purifying rooms of the stale odours of human habitation. Windows became wider and bigger to accommodate the new drive to circulate fresh air. It must have been a huge improvement on the overwhelming fug that had bred so many bed bugs, but more often than not it just made rooms draughty rather than fresh and clean. According to the French writer Odette Keun, who lived in London in the 1930s: 'it is true that the English windows, whether they are open or closed, all let in the air anyway; they all rattle; and their panes are all opaquely grey'.

While it is true that bad smells are often signs of mould, decay or stagnation, the smell of cleanliness is no longer the smell of nothing at all, the odour-free sign of an object or person being simply themselves. The smell of cleanliness has to be proof of the process of

KEEPING THINGS AIRY: Books, if they are left untouched, are prone to mould. Never push a book to the back of the shelf; make sure it has air front and back. In the days when houses were spring-cleaned every year, books were taken out one by one, rubbed gently with a damp cloth, dried and put back. If their bindings were leather, they were given some leather polish.

cleaning. Neatly combining miasma theory and germ theory, homes became viewed as laboratories of hygiene whose inhabitants were always on the lookout for both odours and bacteria. From the late nineteenth century, there was a passion for disinfectant smelling heavily of carbolic that would kill these intruders in a single wipe. The stench it left behind was proof of a job well done: for a century, the smell of carbolic was the very essence of punitively healthy domestic sanitation.

Boiling, fumigating and dosing with disinfectants were now part of the household duties. Lydia Balderson's 1936 *Housewifery: A Textbook of Practical Housekeeping* laid down a terrifying list of must-dos. 'Every housewife must be acquainted with disinfectants and fumigants, because drains, garbage cans, and ice boxes need them; and cellars must be kept free from chance causes of odours or sickness.' Balderson recommended regularly cleaning the 'flush closet' with strong doses of washing soda, chloride of lime or potassium permanganate, and daily cleaning with soap and water and a brush. Dishcloths should be washed after every dishwashing and kitchen towels boiled two or three times a week for five minutes, with soap.

Balderson was one of many authors to echo a new theme in advice books on housekeeping: keeping a home clean had become a science – associated not only with hygiene and new theories of health but with the science of

JOY DETERGENT AND ARTIFICIAL SMELLS: By the 1950s, the smell of cleanliness came in all sorts of different fragrances. The American bacteriologist Theodor Rosebury, reminding his readers that it is only when human secretions decompose that they actually smell, lamented: 'We have become a nation of tubbed, scrubbed, deodorised neurotics.' It was the vast popularity of Coco Chanel's perfume No. 5, launched in 1921 and incorporating chemical fragrances for the first time, that persuaded detergent manufacturers of the marketing potential of smell. The once ubiquitous odour of carbolic was replaced by laboratory created alpine breezes, freshly cut lawns and whiffs of pine. In 1966, a survey found that the addition of a lemon scent to Joy detergent successfully convinced consumers that it was superior to a scentless one, despite the fact that the actual substance of the detergent was unaltered: this was attributed to consumers' association of cleaning with the grease-cutting ability of real lemon.

management itself. Because germs were an invisible enemy, everywhere but undetectable, strong smelling soaps and cleaning fluids indicated purification where no proof of it was visible to the naked eye. Manufacturers rushed to develop sprays, soaps and detergents that could accommodate every different kind of cleansing need. In the past,

the cleaning of the house was satisfactorily completed with basic soap and water. Now a host of different products were required – each advertising their own fragrance.

Vinegar was a traditional method of keeping nasty odours at bay. Put a bowl of vinegar in a smelly room for

LIMESCALE is the bane of hard water areas. But it's so easy to remove with vinegar or citric acid as to be almost miraculous. There is no need at all to buy expensive specialist limescale removers for which you need to wear goggles and rubber gloves. Fill your kettle with half a cup of vinegar topped up with water and leave overnight. Next morning, boil the kettle, empty it and watch the flakes of limescale disappear down the plug hole. Fill the kettle with clear water and boil again. Citric acid is, if anything, even more effective. Half a teaspoon in a kettleful of water will eradicate any traces of limescale completely. Half a cup of citric acid poured into the drum of washing machines or dishwashers (don't put it in the soap dispensers) and the machine then turned to the hottest cycle will keep your pipes blissfully clear of flaky limescale deposits.

a few hours and it will soak up the whiffs. Owners of the first refrigerators were advised to sprinkle vinegar or bicarbonate of soda at the bottom of the vegetable drawers to keep them fresh.

BICARBONATE OF SODA is useful for absorbing unwanted smells. If you want to get rid of the smell of cigarette smoke from a room, leave a bowl of bicarbonate there overnight and it will help soak them up.

TIP!

MOULD AND MILDEW: Rub vinegar around the seal of your washing machine door every week to soak up the black slime deposited by liquid detergents. Dilute one cup vinegar with three cups of water and use for removing mildew from grouting in bathrooms. A spray of it now and then will stop mildew forming.

Afterword

Ce qu'on verra au Salon des Arts ménagers
pas encore, mais bientôt

L'ELECTRO-SERVICE
Avec lui, au moins, pas d'indiscrétions

Dessin de FABIANO.

Houses are to live in, not to look at
Francis Bacon

OUR FANTASIES OF THE FUTURE generally feature homes that are conspicuously liberated from the drudgery of day-to-day domestic labour. We envisage biddable robots, self-cleaning clothes, compostable furniture and meals created from a handful of nutritious pills. But so far, despite being encouraged by inventors and science fiction to believe that this utopia is just around the corner, most human societies show a marked reluctance to let go of the old idea of home as a place of mess, clutter and accumulation. Not many people actually want to inhabit the machine for living in which was promised by modernist architects a century ago. The aesthetic of cosiness and clutter, of cushions and squashy sofas and dust-collecting curtains, has refused to go away and has even increased in popularity. Homes still require maintenance – household goods are still besieged by the problems of damp, stains and pests. No one has yet, for example, come up with a really foolproof way of getting rid of moths that doesn't involve an explosion of toxic chemicals and require you to leave the house for three days.

And yet, although we spend far less time cleaning our houses than most of our forebears a century ago, we also seem to have made it a great deal more complicated. A dozen different kinds of chemical sprays, for bathrooms, for kitchens, for wooden furniture, for windows, for computer screens, could be happily replaced by a gallon container of distilled vinegar. Add some bicarbonate of soda to get a scrub going and perhaps some borax as a grease dissolver, and you have all you need to clean your home cheaply, efficiently and without the synthetic odour of artificial pine.

Few people now would actually want to live like an Edwardian housemaid – but the skills of a career servant can come in useful for cleaning an old mirror

or freshening up a gilt picture frame. Now that we don't fight the grim everyday battle against coal smuts, cleaning a bathroom using only the juice of a single lemon – and a bit of spit and polish – holds its own small satisfaction.

Acknowledgements

WITH THANKS TO Catherine Clarke and George Lucas for getting the ball rolling and to Michael Fishwick at Bloomsbury and Amy Cherry at W. W. Norton for picking it up with such alacrity. Thanks too Polly Napper and Holly Ovenden at Bloomsbury whose visual flair created the wonderful text and cover designs; to Catherine Best for reading the proofs and to David Atkinson for compiling the index; to Marigold Atkey and above all to Anna Simpson whose keen eye for detail and infectious enthusiasm made working on the book together a real pleasure. Without her this book would never have been finished.

Image Credits

88   Pear's advertisement, 1922, The Print Collector / Print
Collector / Getty Images

90   Pedestal wash-down closets, Science & Society Picture
Library / SSPL / Getty Images

95   View of the Procter & Gamble production line where
employees bottle Joy dish detergent, 1950, Cincinnati
Museum Center / Getty Images

97   Cleaning products on supermarket shelves, 1966, Paul
Walters Worldwide Photography Ltd. / Heritage Images /
Getty Images

100   A discreet robot servant brings a breakfast tray to a lady in
bed, Mary Evans Picture Library

Index

Lucy Lethbridge has written for a number of publications and is also the author of several children's books, one of which, *Who Was Ada Lovelace?*, won the 2002 Blue Peter Award for non-fiction. *Servants: A Downstairs View of Twentieth-century Britain* was published to critical acclaim by Bloomsbury in 2012. She lives in London.

A NOTE ON THE TYPE

The text of this book is set in Adobe Caslon, named after the English punch-cutter and type-founder William Caslon I (1692–1766). Caslon's rather old-fashioned types were modelled on seventeenth-century Dutch designs, but found wide acceptance throughout the English-speaking world for much of the eighteenth century until replaced by newer types towards the end of the century. Used in 1776 to print the Declaration of Independence, they were revived in the nineteenth century and have been popular ever since, particularly amongst fine printers. There are several digital versions, of which Carol Twombly's Adobe Caslon is one.